DECLARATION
OF INTERDEPENDENCE:

Advocate Poetically!

J.S. CHRISTIAN

AuthorHouse™
1663 Liberty Drive
Bloomington, IN 47403
www.authorhouse.com
Phone: 1 (833) 262-8899

Because of the dynamic nature of the Internet, any web addresses or links contained in this book may have changed since publication and may no longer be valid. The views expressed in this work are solely those of the author and do not necessarily reflect the views of the publisher, and the publisher hereby disclaims any responsibility for them.

Any people depicted in stock imagery provided by Getty Images are models, and such images are being used for illustrative purposes only.
Certain stock imagery Getty Images.

This book is printed on acid-free paper.

ISBN: 978-1-6655-0496-6 (sc)
ISBN: 978-1-6655-0495-9 (hc)
ISBN: 978-1-6655-0497-3 (e)

Library of Congress Control Number: 2020920748

Print information available on the last page.

Published by AuthorHouse 12/09/2020

authorHOUSE®

PREFACE

Art with a conflict resolution voice. Declarations...has a wide range of advocacy expressions; mostly human. In Book III an obscured tree appreciates "Quin-treessential" acknowledgement and disgruntled "Furniture" join a protest. A "Resolution" depiction advocates for civility and health. "Just Like You" Enforcement in Book IV points out we are more "headaches and heartaches" alike than different.

Creative fictitious depictions dapple in historical topics like education injustices and hate crimes in "Carlsbad Decree Lament" and plights of Native Americans in "Nothing New for Sioux". Enforcement has a voice in "Comply" and "Chosen Outfits".

Declaration looks through lenses of both the observer and observed. "Just in Case" and "Swimming Lessons" cry out for educational accountability. The "Hearty Farmer" simply could care less.

ABOUT THE AUTHOR

"Let's Talk"

While the world was in quarantine, J. S. Christian was creatively penning a passion for justice, education, and resolution. Declaration was born from a spirit of hope for America.

The former military officer and U.S. Naval Academy English Literature instructor is also a Pepperdine University School of Law alum. The Atlanta native currently resides with family on the west coast.

xxxxxxxxxxxxxxxxxxxxxxxx

J.S. Christian

CONTENTS

Advocate Unity

Advocate School Reform

Advocate Of Mental Wealth

Advocate Enforcement

Veterans Pray

Love

Advocate Unity

J.S. Christian

DECLARATION OF INTERDEPENDENCE

In accordance with the U.S. Constituted...

Declaration.

The one drop rule and 5/5ths men now

Emancipated.

We are all multicolored

Indivisibly a nation.

Clearly enunciated.

Undergoing reparation

®

2

J.S. Christian

PROETRY

Proetry: poetic protest
outcry language script.

When we say more in fewer words
All better handle it.

Offended ears block messages.
F- bombs impact the kids.

Civility must reign to show what unifying did

Proetry evokes.
It's not just here to entertain.

Proetry calls to action every faction of the game.

This one calls out a shout to all who wrote in revolutions

Understanding unifying is the only resolution

When we...

V. oice

O. ur

T. houghts

E. lectorally

It's then and how we are heard.
Put your fingerprint on history.
Is electorally even a word?

LET'S TALK

I don't know how to talk to you
I do know what to say
I have unsown seeds for fertile soil
I want to spread your way

I long to make
Connections

Together forward
We should step

Please see my heart
So we can start
Our country needs the help

To heal our pain,
Unite again
before we fall apart

I don't know how to talk to you
I know this is a start

CONNECTIONS

When you break connect i o n s

You

      l o s e

         P

             O

             W

             e

             r

J.S. Christian

HIGHER CONSTRUCT

We hold these truths of having
Been created equal tightly

In so doing, we remind ourselves in prayer
daily and nightly

Focus on goodness, self rely
Self sustain, boldly cry

Be true to who and how God made you stand

Educate where lessons come
Never hold out flattened palms
To beg
Instead rotate to shake a hand

(Your brothers hand)

Only look down
To tie your shoes and to teach young
Children who

Look up to you
As good women
And men

Seek favor only from above
Love all people. Receive love.
Again.

J.S. Christian

SOCIAL CONSTRUCT

It's not that we don't want you here
We just don't want to see you

Or talk to you
Or walk with you
And certainly not free you

From the burden of oppression
Or the onset of depression

That ensues
Ostracizing is much easier
We've worked too hard to be here

To not work hard
To not see you here too

NO ONE KNOCKED

It may take a minute
Or 500 years
to recover.
This was our land
Not yours to
"Discover"

J.S. Christian

GOOD GUY

He is not God
so why the
trembling?
He is not God
so why the
fear?

He's just a man
who has no plan to hurt you.

He's huge, that's true
Though so are you

With what it is you

Plan to do
To hurt him.

When you call to cause alarm

See your father
See your son

See our Father and His son

See a man there who has...

No plans to hurt you.

J.S. Christian

COLOR BLIND

When you claim to see no color

It makes me scratch my head.

Driving must be hard for you

No green, yellow, or red.

NEWS FLASH!

There are some Whites who are not millionaires.

In fact, there are many on public welfare.

Who are not racists, lying hatefuls chasing others out of town.

Who could care less whose car is best or that your skin is brown.

We have bills, also get chills when flashing lights go by

And pray today is not the day another young Black man will die.

J.S. Christian

UGLY REFLECTIONS

I can't help you think I'm ugly
You have to work that out yourself.
What I can see inside of me is
Lovely Gracious Boundless Wealth.

Puckering lips, this skin these hips
were formed and coated.
Chiseled. Hued.
By God. My God. Our God. Oh God!

Though this I offer you.
Who look at me and, ugly, see
A scowling grimace or a frown
Reflection
(no judgment here)
Faced your way, Dear.
I'll kindly put the mirror down.

FOLD OVER

I try to never confuse
Who I am
With
With
Who I am
They are not the same

J.S. Christian

RACE WAR

Color yourself a canter of inspirational songs
Want to hear
have hearts endear
In rhythm
Want to
Move along.
(race war is suicide)
Sing songs, play music.
Listen.
Of divine Genesis foreborne.
Purge all hate before too late.
Before too long
Before too worn.
(race war is suicide)
So hum the hymns of hers and his and theirs and ours
because all are
Of ours and theirs and Hers and His
Keyboarded Picked Percussioned Drummed
Plucked oh so gently Melodicas gentry
Autotune caress and strum

Intertwined and intermittent
Implausible to pull apart

Keyboards and kids and kinds of threads
That bind our bodies and our hearts
(race war is suicide)
Melodies can't be dissected
Songs just as notes will clang and die
Divide us. Full stop.
Stop the music.
SILENCE?
Race war is suicide.
Race war is suicide.
Let's choose to live and love another
Day by day
Brother by brother.

J.S. Christian

SOME BLACK BOYS

Some Black boys see some Black girls
as pretty
They like them and then both
grow up to be.
Some Black men who see
Black women soulmates.
Wait, pray some
Beautifully marry.

SOME WHITE BOYS

Some White boys see some
White girls as pretty.
They know them and then
both grow up to be.
Some White Men
who see White women as family
Then protect, propose and marry naturally

HYPO-

When I stand with my right fist
Held high in the air
While left hand
and fingers
Twirl through my dyed hair.
I cry out "injustice!"
And wide-leg stance stand
Then fob-lock my import and
Sanitize my hands.
After shaking the others' and
Selfie with the crowd
Then post on to Twitter.
These folks are so loud!
I am bailing so hailing a cab
Out of here.
I've done social justice and
Snapped it. Sincere.

J.S. Christian

NO BIG DEAL

I'm Asian and my wife is Black.

It's really no big deal
Race plays no part
How either of us feel

I saw her. She was very cute. Also very smart
Her gorgeous smile drew me in, quickly melted my heart
The best thing about her
There are many I can see
Is that she also chose to fall
in love with me

INSIDER

When you live inside
Whale's belly,
You see
Wha
Whe

Who
He eats

Just prior to digested self
once a delicious treat

CHOCOLATE FOR PRESIDENT

Chocolate croissants as ballots
Sprinkles along with Tweets

Rocky road en route to polls
Sundaes each day of the week.

Brownie Pizza slices as convention lunch
Would bring out every sweet tooth

Fudge U.S. to happy bunch.

Yellow cake and chocolate frosting
White chocolate is great!

What gets the vote is mocha floats
No need for a debate.

Chocolate is bipartisan, so all it represents
The sweetest choices are delicious voices

Chocolate for President!

STEREOS

Not all of them are like that
I've met a few who don't.

Some I've seen will do those things
Though some certainly won't.

When you say "they" name two
or more for evidence or else,

You exaggerate and overstate.
Just wasting precious breath.

Base any 'they' on hearsay and you are surely wrong
Or just prejudice and need to change
yourself, your views, that song

JUSTICE SCOUT RECRUIT

I believe in playing ball so, on the cause, I'm sold.

However, if you want me on your team this must unfold:

1. Approach me real and proper. Make your message clear.
2. Don't shout. This turns me off. There's a chance that I won't hear.
3. Do your homework. Know yourself. Know exactly who I am.
4. Don't hit me with a bat. This hurts us both; it kills the plan.
5. Have and share your vision of my role on your team.
6. Use sincere semantics clearly stating what you mean.

That's it. Just this. Commit.

Phone in and I will take your call.

The country says move quickly.

Let's play ball!

J.S. Christian

Justice Scout Recruit

RESOLUTION

All

BLM, too.

There,

fixed it.

Won the battle. Knocked on doors. The world answered. Now what's next?

**Know the pen is as powerful
a punch as any fis**t

Come inside

Don't lose more lives;
this war
U.S. came too far for this

Time to *demonstrate*

What matters

Most throughout
the whole country

UNITED HEALTHY

forward moving

ALL TOGETHER
FAITHFULLY

J.S. Christian

VIRTUALLY IMPERSONAL

Before asking

How was your day?

We first see what social media says.

Sitting at dinner no engagement no doubt.

Minds are totally focused out.

Bonding with a virtual never met

on the other side of the screen.

While human on the other side

of the table is waiting to be seen.

COMPATIBLE

We can agree on many things
Though I'm fries, you onion rings.
We both prefer our coffee without cream
I'm a vegan
You eat meat
Neither like the middle seat.
When we don't know the words to songs, we fake them.
I like water, you snow ski
I am Jewish
You, Hindi
As sports go, we both can leave or take them
I'm a seltzer, you drink coke
Neither laugh at racist jokes
Or make them

J.S. Christian

TRASH TALKING

Amounts of land aren't infinite.
Amounts of trash certainly are
It's not acknowledged as a crisis
At least not so far

We need somewhere to put all of our dry bones and
All the trash we all like to produce
Or plan to live on scented hills,
Plan to mass olfactory kill.
And never ever plan
To reproduce.

NIMBY

You can't see us in the attics
Basements are too dark and dank.
We can't remember how we got here
Though are sure who should be thanked

All the

N.ot-
I.n-
M.y-
B.ack-
Y.arders

Wanting us to disappear
We have a right
to have a life and
Live anywhere
but here.

J.S. Christian

FIRST PLAQUES

I'm Hispanic
I don't understand why we still denote 1st Blacks
I know it's meant to celebrate.
I just need some more facts

Are we proud of their accomplishments
Or the fact they were held back?
for so many years so firsts are really 'See Suppression' plaques?

I was born here. It gets questioned.
Sanchez is my family name.
But 1st Blacks are Smiths and Washingtons
We all know where they came...

from what I've seen, the 1st Blacks descend direct your seed

So "1st Blacks of Our Family" is how the plaques should read

DANCERS

Want to see something funny?
Watch me dance. Oh my.
I enjoy the music. Moving.
Mentally. I try.

If square dancing's what we're doing
then I'm trying to dosey doe
If we're waltzing then I'm boxing
probably stepping on your toes

I can two-step with enough prep
make it look good in the dark
Or just chair dance in my khaki pants
Wave my arms and bark.

Sure, laugh when you see moves and music
mostly out of sync.
Too left/right leaners dance bad as we think!

J.S. Christian

PLOTTERS

As you moved closer we thought
you were being friendly
As you moved closer we assumed
that you were kind

Now we can better see
Your steps were only meant to be
used as markers noting
"all of yours is mine"

Seen exactly where you stand

From where we stood
all of your scales and
measures could
use recalibration.

You were all off.

A misunderstanding

was any cause

for celebration.

J.S. Christian

HEARTY FARMER

Greg was a hearty farmer with lots of land to care.
Uncomplicated. Unencumbered.
Just wheat and steer out there.

Farm traffic had no stoplights
Tractor drivers never yelled.
He sped 10 miles per hour
rolling
rolling
up hay bales.

To communicate with cattle he didn't have to text
There were never social battles.
He really could care less.
His hearty seeds made feed
some vegetables,
for food
and then

He'd grab a hearty handful.

Start the process o'er again.

And again.

And again.

J.S. Christian

NOT FUNNY; OFFENSIVE

Were your parents married?
Is that your real hair?
Did you go to college?
Did you finish?
If so, where?

And how? Athletic scholarship?
How do you speak so well?
Chatting with you on the phone, you know I could hardly tell?

Oh, you're not just visiting?
Do you own or rent?
Just curious how you pay for things.
How funds are earned and spent.

Your kids, are they adopted?
Do they have the same dad?
Hey, where are you going?!
You seem mad.

(MARTIN) AND LEWIS REUNION

(Well, welcome!
You look good, John!
Got Vivian with you!

Oh goodness, here's the young bucks
Our 'get in good trouble' crew)

J.S. Christian

Ah, hush, now you're just saying that
You came when you were young.

Sorry how you got here, man.
That whole thing was so wrong.

(What thing?! I'm good.
go look around
No shots or crying here.

We have the best seats in the house
to watch young bucks down there)

Hope they look up, check in with us with Father THEN go act

Remember right beats wrong and good is cancelled out by bad,

(lies are cancelled out by facts)

Balance social justice, rights, and rightfully fighting for it.

Know good trouble's
within the law now
and never dare ignore this.

(Yeah, was really tough so rough
for us and some of our allies)

(Martin) and Lewis Reunion

The bridges, marches, dreams and ditches. Hope there's an 'other side'.

So, Martin,

(What?)

One question,

does ...

He show favoritism?

(Absolutely!

In due time

sure does,

for ALL of His children.

J.S. Christian

(Martin) and Lewis Reunion

U.

S.

A.

UNIFIED

State of America

What does the flag cover art symbolize?

Middle School art project winner. Declarations of Interdependence; Advocate Poetically!
The 15 stripes represent the Voting Rights 15th Amendment. There are 51 stars. The
51st purple star represents Purple Hearts, (bipartisan Washington, DC) and the
U. nified S.tate of A.merica

J.S. Christian

Advocate School Reform

JUST IN CASE

JUST IN CASE
They can't play Basketball.
Or run fast
Around the track at all.
Or sing and dance
Let's take a chance.
And educate our kids.
JUST IN CASE
A chase to catch
Falls short
Of the scouter's match for any sport.
Let's academically work out.
And educate our kids.

J.S. Christian

**When math and science
clearly seem.
The best recruiter and best team**

Let's shift implicit bias back
Include all students
And all facts
Please EDUCATE ALL KIDS.

RESUSCITATION

Sometimes,
I can't breathe
So I have to

grab a Pen
To
Exhale

J.S. Christian

SWIMMING LESSONS

Since I'm from Atlanta, I know Martin's brother drowned.
Then Dr. Has-a-Cure from Harvard
Was just nowhere to be found
(he drowned)
LESSONS. Swimming lessons
Lessen anti-buoyancy

As a brother then a scientist
Are helping us to see.
Increasing swimming lessons
Increase opportunities
For creative budding scholars'
DNA commodities
LESSONS. Swimming lessons,
Pulsate hearts so hope can thrive.
Keeping brothers, doctors, scientists
aFLOAT aWOKE aLIVE

J.S. Christian

MISSING SCHOLAR

Can you help me find Samantha? She sat in that seat right there.
A small Brown girl with dark brown curls
Disappeared into thin air.
Can we try to reach Samantha? Can you tell me where she went?

She came to school like other kids

To learn, to grow, to mark present.

Caboose. Never line leader. Went out last and held the doors.
While classmates laughed and socialized. She did the classroom chores.
She never missed the parties
She was not invited to.
Learned protocol that all means all
means everyone but you.
"Samantha banana brown girl from Havana" Actually hailed from Carlsbad
always ignored and quite often bored.
The bullying made her quite sad.

Ashley P. to the left drew mean faces. Ashley K. did the same on the right
Both invited, included and full attitude.
Found fun in provoking to fight.
Samantha always raised her hand first.

To answer the questions. Compete.

Against Ashley, just one, who enjoyed making fun

As they sat in the star gifted seats.
Samantha's zeal was marginalized quickly
Then disordered as ADHD.
While Ashley's was lauded and often applauded preclusion to a PhD.
Samantha one day just stopped coming
rest assured what it's all about
Scholar oxymoron coercion
Ensures all smart brown students get out.
Can you help me find Samantha ?

POETIC PULSE

Poetry
requires readers
to breathe.

Without
Readers
Poetry
Has no Pulse.

NO RIGHT TO EDUCATION

Brown v. new brown generation
New musicians misspelling same songs,
Educashun
Educasion
EDUCATION
is a
Privilige
Privalage
Priveledge

Privileged **PRIVILEGE**
Not Right; some try
With disabled deny
How could this ever go wrung?

J.S. Christian

LESSONS LEARNED

You teach me
like you like me
I learn like
You teach me
to like me too.

You teach me
like you hate me
and I learn like
You teach me
to hate me. And you...

who holds the keys to
knowledge, academics,
cards to college

who to and who not to listen to

You taught me
the opposite
of what not
loving learning
could be.

Signed,
a former student,
PhD

AXIOMS

Hate requires action
to become a verb.
Silence cannot be misquoted.
Mirrors reflect.
Hearts can detect...
When childhood dreams are Imploded.

J.S. Christian

TORTOISE V. SHELLED HARE

In the ongoing case of Shell-less Tortoise v. Shelled Hare

Starting line is wide and level
Starting guns startle some there

BANG!

Course knowledge undiluted at the start. Fair as it should

Determining determination. Str8 paths and through the woods.

Then course markers noticed punctures on the Tortoise back

where cover was removed at times along the arduous track

The shell had dents and paw prints. Graffiti "you're too slow!"

Tortoises can't talk. There was no way for us to know.

The hare used as umbrella then, Tortoise shell, as shield...

To protect and project himself.

Your Honor, help us if you will.

"In due time.
Race is in Progress.
The jury is out still."

HUSH

People with something to say

Often don't in fear

Someone may be listening
To what everyone should
hear.

J.S. Christian

MATH TEST

M ake A ccountable T o H onor

T eaching
E very
S tudent
T ruth

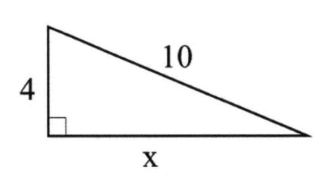

$$a^2 + b^2 = c^2$$

$$4^2 + x^2 = 10^2$$

$$16 + x^2 = 100$$

$$\underline{-16 \qquad\quad -16}$$

$$x^2 = 84$$

$$x = \sqrt{84}$$

$$x \approx 9.2$$

ASSIMILATION

I tried on assimilation.
They did not have one in my size.
All t's were crossed
Lanes never were
And I seldom rolled my eyes.
They looked straight
as did my hair
As long and often as I could.
Then I saw
It did not matter
All efforts were.
misunderstood.
Fitting whatever
caricature
Of the character
last seen
I say no thanks.
Not anymore.
That outfit's just not
right for me.

J.S. Christian

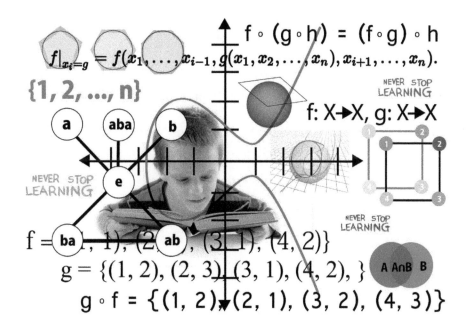

$$f \circ (g \circ h) = (f \circ g) \circ h$$

$$f|_{x_i=g} = f(x_1, \ldots, x_{i-1}, g(x_1, x_2, \ldots, x_n), x_{i+1}, \ldots, x_n).$$

$$\{1, 2, \ldots, n\}$$

NEVER STOP LEARNING

$$f: X \to X, \; g: X \to X$$

NEVER STOP LEARNING

NEVER STOP LEARNING

$$f = \{(1, 1), (2, 3), (3, 1), (4, 2)\}$$

$$g = \{(1, 2), (2, 3), (3, 1), (4, 2), \}$$

$$g \circ f = \{(1, 2), (2, 1), (3, 2), (4, 3)\}$$

A AnB B

Count them in and
things could happen
Count them out and
you're in trouble
Count them wrong
you have to ask them
Exactly which box
do you bubble?

Count as 1/2 or 1/2 then double?

RETORT

Julie hated losing. She punched the new Black
girl named Kay.

Kay was smarter, cute, and witty though
was unsure just what to say.

When Julie called her the n- word,
it echoed around the world

Kay was silent,
taught non-violence,
so didn't hit the the girl

(On the playground)

Kay stood still in contemplation

then replied with a retort

J.S. Christian

"Middle school has kiddie rules.
I'll see you one day in my court."

CARLSBAD DECREE LAMENT

Carlsbad circa 1819.
Brotherhoods all in collusion.
News and students muffled or caste out.

School bells should have warnings. Truth for all would be
alarming
what Carlsbad's Decree was all about.

J.S. Christian

What if we pay our taxes?
What if we mow our lawn?

What if I
What if I
What if I
What if I

Tell you that I'm unarmed?

What if I bring you bundt cakes?
What if I wave hello?

What if I
What if I
What if I
What if I

Tell you that we all know...

Some of your long-held secrets...
Most of your long told lies.

Choosing to vengeance bully
Means educate deny

Why won't you
Why won't you
Why won't you

Why can't you

Look us all in the eyes?

How can we be your neighbor?
How can you not cause harm?

Why must we
Stay away
Why must you
Why must they

Always look so alarmed?

Why when some kids test "gifted"
Scrutiny must be done?

Smart; too much
Smart though just
Hue's askew.
Legal thrust.

There has to be something wrong.

**no IDEA why disabled. pay for those who mislabel. and your own.
this is wrong. going on. way too long. Violate IDEA; hurt.**

Why do you down diversing?
Why do you hate-crime fight?

How do you
How do you
How do you
How do you

How do you sleep at night?

You're gonna call this fiction
Seems you can't handle facts

What do you
What do you
What do you
What do you

What do you think of that?

HIDE N' SEEK

When you close your eyes we still see you.
Prolonged
Doing so
You can see
Us in
Nightmares
And Dreams.
The best thing it seems
Is to wake up and stay woke.
Knowing...

We're not going away.
Here we are
Here we'll stay
This is no time to play
Hide and Seek.

J.S. Christian

COME WITH LANTERNS

Hold up a light to the darkness.
In darkness the shady ones live
Prey on the weak
Label as freaks
To take and to take and not give.
Let's shed some light on these bad guys.
Call them cowardly. Victims. Make cry.

When they're caught, isolate as the spreaders of hate.
Place labels and don't even try.
To include them with all of the non-bullies.
Then name call. Cheer angst and pick fights.
Grab your lanterns, go get them!
Stop them, don't forget them!
Reflect bullying isn't right.
(By bullying?)

HANDY CAP

Fund tether them tightly.
Reach out and hold.

Teach them the ways.
Give means to grow old.
Handicapped children
grow up to be
Handicapped grown ups
who still are in need.

J.S. Christian

PARENTAL GUIDANCE

Kids used to play outside.

A lot of other kids were there.
Some fun was there was
Little parental supervision.

Kids are now back inside

Friends have video games,
virtual bonds with strangers,
F- bombs,
N- words, swastikas.
Little Parental Guidance.

No worries.

At least they're safe.

THANKSTAKING

It's our fault
We won't blame you.
We should have felt the
snake oil on your hands.
Little cause for celebration
Used, abused, then forsaken.
Now we see
exactly where you stand.

On our land.

J.S. Christian

CHOKEHOLDS

What is the return
on the investment
For placing chokeholds on opportunities.
Starting at the onset
of formal education.
How is it no one can seem to see
just what this does
to the entire nation?
There are places educators are
held in high esteem
And there are others who have no
idea what esteem even means

FLIGHT 380 TO BIRMINGHAM

she was, when it happened,
neither for nor against.
just napping...

because she could.

they were, when it happened,
neither for nor against.
all laughing...

as children should.

she was, when it happened,
missing kids bible study because the 380 delay
then **bump!** plane landed
then **boom!** church exploded

she was grateful her plane arrived late.

J.S. Christian

Flight 380 to Birmingham

NOTHING NEW FOR SIOUX

We spoke in two different languages.
We spoke from two different hearts.
You felt entitled to stay, kill and take

We wanted you to depart.
You called it Manifest Destiny
We called it heartless and cold.
The trails of tears terrors and fears
Nothing settled
STOLE.

J.S. Christian

DEAR KINDER,

Little Scholar Riley
Can you go run me an errand?
You're much younger
will be stronger
and can reach
Much further in the future
As you go, I can ensure
you'll grow dendrites
From the lessons that I teach.
Grab a crayon, take some notes.
Never take for granted
rote,
or the

Abacus or any boring speech
I'm just laying
the foundation
for you to grow
and run...
THE NATION
standing on
learning
lessons
that I teach

J.S. Christian

WINNING MINDS

When intellect contradicts melanin content;

B.S. Oxymoron. Oh my!

If a few are let in then supremacy ends

And equality may go awry.

Man your stations, coasts, schools, and your status

Scholars rise above walls and gates

Armed with the Almighty's Handbook of Highering.

"Winning! Putting love against hate"

AFFIRMATIVE (DISTR)ACTION

Imagine running 10 extra miles to the start
of a marathon.

You painstakingly
complete all 36.2

However,
your finish
Is forever
marginalized
Due to the color
of your shoes.

(yeah, it's like that)

J.S. Christian

DEAF EDUCATION

She says she wants to make a living.
You want her to make a sign.
We're thinking education.
You're just mocking, marking time.
We hear depth and intellect.
Researching classes at Yale.
You have hate on speed dial
to take from schools to fail.
We know of aspirations.
Big future dreams and goals.
You're counting down 'til she's
18 years old.

82   *J.S. Christian*

RINDS

The tough outer coating
of sweetness inside.
Projecting and flavoring
all over time.
Decide how the future will taste

Protecting, impacting
fragile young minds
Imagine the impact
the future will find.
In fruit juiced with kindness not hate.

U.

S.

A.

UNIFIED

State of America

Middle School flag art winner. Declarations of Interdependence; Advocate Poetically! square flag is equal4 all sides. The 15 stripes, 51-star flag art represents the 15th Amendment Voting Rights. Purple 51st star represents both Purple Hearts and the Washington, D.C. newly **U.nified S.tate of A.merica.**

STEALING BASES

Heaven help the Robbing Hooders
Who by day chant songs of praise

Of themselves for all the hard work
and e-funds they selfless raise

For their own kids' school tuition
Disabled children's caste aside

Faking CARE now camera rolling.
Then misappropriate. Tell lies.

Making jokes of kid's expressions
Mocking movements to frustrate

Casting shame on least amongst
US. Should repent before too late

MATURITY

Unashamed of her behavior
Unaware when coming on
Though some staff will
sadly laugh
just like the students poking fun
The more mature are empathetic
understanding neurons fail.
Disabled need more understanding
not laughter, ableism, jail.
The more mature were empathetic
sympathetic unafraid
To stand apart and stand up for then
stand against what others said.

J.S. Christian

HYPOTHESIS

Sparking ideas fuels ambitions
Crushing ideals is foreboding

Mirrors reflect
Truth
with respect

To childhood dreams
as exploding

J.S. Christian

MEMES SCHOOL

Glancing at the seating charts in newly reformed schools.
Still in alpha order. Very confusing rules.

No pictures. Confidential.

No cameras. Minors there.

Can't reform the old way
with germs everywhere!

Let's just meme them,
make it all seem fair.

Advocate Of
Mental Wealth

IT'S OKAY

Sometimes it's OK
To not be OK
Acceptable not to be fine.
To need just a minute
To not be with it.
To want just a little more time...
To be OK.

J.S. Christian

BREAKTHROUGH

I did Catholicism easily
it taught me how to Guilt

And patience was a piece of cake
it's how Rome was built

Great Wall of China - easy climb was just a little hill
Decathlons. Yeah bring em on!
Just 10 sports slots to fill

but success?
oh, what a mess!
a challenge
just a dream

I can't seem to master that

Don't know what it means

I go out and up and down

Then back to 'my place'

All because I'm wearing

a brown face.

NEW NEW SOUTH

Grady of The New South cries out

"now it is your turn!"

This place is trying to slip apart
go show them what you learned

That left and right and
north and south
are far more than directions

And we can't run a whole country
divided into sections

By now we should face forward
not backwards have to look

for resolution lessons
chronicled in history books.

The U.S. is us and us U.S. in the U.S.A.
Fifty parts together have to operate that way

And colors? Do they matter?
You best believe they do.

J.S. Christian

Our banners fly in bright
Red, White and Blue

All colors? Yes, they matter!
You best believe they do.

Aside flag flying Higher -
Red, White, Blue

WHENSDAY?

I need to schedule a day for a break down
Next Tuesday at 10 just won't do.
Cause between now and then the *subscription will end.
I don't know if I want to renew

The Monday before is my off day.
Having then would be awkward and bleak.
It would just be absurd.
And who's ever heard of a breakdown beginning the week?

The Sunday before? Holy heck no!
Guilt alone would just reel me back in.
I'm not bearing the cross when comparing my loss
To life that for me came to an end.

All Saturday I will be solo since the world takes this day to have fun.
And I'll be here inside having all day cold cried,
First responders go bask in warm sun.
Friday 315 is a maybe.
Traffic is just starting to slow.
Then cause me all would stop and rush-hour would not.
Rush will be to do, well, we all know.

Thursday 640 could happen.
By then caring friends will all be home.
But, oh wait, no they won't, no they can't, no they don't.

J.S. Christian

Reality is I have none.
So that just leaves tomorrow and Wednesday
The most boring-ist days of them all.

Now have given more thought, I do know that I ought
go soon humbly and answer this call.
When and if I come back, I'll...

ARRIVED

I will have arrived
When
Those who have
Neither
Seen me in
Nor Changed
My diapers
Praise my work.
Unsolicited.

J.S. Christian

LOOK AT ME

I sat next to you

on the train today.
You weren't quite sure
just what to say.
To me sitting here
chatting with myself.
Did you not here
my cry for help?
I looked around to
see if you
could here the noises,
popping too.
I'm guessing no.
You moved away.
You weren't quite sure
just what to say.

J.S. Christian

HELP

Here's how can address
our off-shoots...

Our loose cannons.

Our off-handed.

Our impaired.

Not write them off
but care enough
to see them as people.
If DARE.

(go help get them

                              some help

                                                        somewhere)

Ask name
share the same
Then sit. Listen.

Silent pause
may just cause
a blank stare

Time to offer a soothing
outreach and affirm
you are sincerely
Present and CARE

J.S. Christian

SPRAY

White friends don't like my friends are Black
Black that my friends are White
My Lefts can't stand that I make plans with ones who are on Right
My hipsters snub my nerdy, my Foodies snub my Cruisers
My kingdom for a magic spray for prejudice diffusers.

QUINT-TREE-CENTRAL

The 5th tree behind
the other four
took just as long to grow
it's just as tall
it's just as thick
Yet other arbors steal the show
The first tree is most visible.
The second gets the breeze.
Tree three can feel
sun glimmers still.
The fourth is within reach.

The fifth is nature's humble fort
stands strong
layers in rings.
Holds blue jays in the wind; sways as the robins perch
to sing.
The fifth's the quintessential
of asking for nothing more
than to be
the only tree
obscured yet clandestine adored.

J.S. Christian

Quint-Tree-Central

IP MY DEFINED

Both Webster® and Cambridge®
say pretty much the same
Try never copy someone else
then claim it with your name
Intellectual means "appealing to
or engaging the intellect"
Property means "things belong
to someone who collects..."
(Stuff)
"My" is far more personal.
Though, here let me define.
It's neither yours nor his nor
theirs, it is quite simply mine.

J.S. Christian

NO ONE

I've never known someone of None.
Created from themselves
Conceived from own seed planted, rooted
grown from No One else.
Yet here we are
Adrift
Afar
Aloft
Alone
Astray

No one's Some of

Someone's son

Detached then blown away.

FURNITURE

Coffee table on all four legs just
upped and walked away.
The sofa slowly followed suit.
You had beans today.

The television looks at you
It's very turned off. Sighs.
You too often change the channel
Based on who you're sitting by.
They're leaving.
You can stand and Tweet.
Entertain yourself by text
Keep treating them like objects,
People next

J.S. Christian

PROSE DOODLE

Color me Kilroy
I reckon.
I suppose.
Beckoned.
Summoned. Begot. Stated.
Written.
(who knows?)

Maybe Chose?

IN LOVE

Too often in love
We fall.
Hard and fast.
With unyielding hearts
And unhealing bruises
and scars.
Unaware of consequences.
Unbridled and disarmed.
For in this battle
The wounding heartless
Take no prisoners
and tend not to play fair.
Too often in love.

J.S. Christian

CARFOOLING

Today I decided to go sit in traffic
to see who humanity are
Timed it just right
so that I might
see the most people and 🚙 cars
Recruited the neighbor to come join the fun, name's either Ellen or Elaine
Though she found it foolish, she agreed to do it.
Actually called it insane.
Driving nowhere...
with someone for nothing (and no one)
Downup 🚙 carpool lane
We felt we were privileged, we got to go faster.
The envy of all of the slow.
Then switched just to show off the fact we had options in which lane we wanted to go
Foregoing the option meant joining the people less environmentally kind
After the 4th deed, all but me could see a gradual losing of mind
So it ended.

A dumb way to go people watch. Carfooling is foolish and lame.
Next time I'll engage in something more human. I'll even go ask what's her name.

J.S. Christian

PEER REVIEWED

I wish that I was more well read,
More couthed,
More cultured,
Better bred.
Designer coiffed and
More well off
So you would read this poem
Knew connoisseurs who doth opine
My depth imbued as well refined
"Renowned prose proven for all times!"
So you would read this poem.
I wish I was related to
The people of the people who
Have credibility so you
Would stop to read my poem
I long for lofty affluence and
Happenings in happenstance
with long stemmed crystal elegance
and readings of my poems.

114

J.S. Christian

I AM

I AM merely a
C
O
M
P
I
L
A
T
I
O
N
of LIVES that HAVE
touched MINE

LIKE IS BLIND

Some White boys see some
Black girls as pretty.
They like them and then
both grow up to be.
Some White men who see
Black women impassioned.
They admire, attach,
Think Love
Propose Marry.

J.S. Christian

BLIND IS LIKE

Some Black boys see some White girls
as pretty
They like them and then both
grow up to be.
Some Black men who see
White women as good choice
They propose, then pray and ask
If will marry.

ASSIMILATION

I tried on assimilation.
They did not have one in my size.
All t's were crossed
Lanes never were
And I seldom rolled my eyes.
They looked straight, as did my hair
As long and often as I could.
Then I saw it did not matter
Efforts were misunderstood.
Fitting whatever caricature
Of the character
last seen.
I say no thanks.
Not anymore.
That outfit's just not
right for me.

J.S. Christian

NOW AND THEN

My ex showed up dressed in all right now.
while I stood all dressed in back then.
His eyes were the same
Same haircut and same name
Even had the same ole
sheepish grin.
He stood unfettered and friendly.
I stood in cracks. Bitter. Down.
I wanted nothing more than to close memories door
And to have him no longer around.
He was armored, care free
and uplifted
by the fact I did not act the same.
I was weighted and burdened, downtrodden in carrying
the burden and brunt of his name.

IN GRIEVING

Forgiveness in grieving is needed
There's a strength gained from
making the shift

From grieving in thoughts
of loved ones we've lost
To calling the memories a gift

Celebrating the stuff of was once there.
Those absent like trophies will set
For revisiting soon.
OK, every blue moon.
We've committed to never forget

Those present who linger - be patient,
The heartaches, the let downs, lost bets.

We graciously say, you may get no display.
We've no place to set you just yet.

J.S. Christian

RESUME'

Perfect imperfection.

Major maker of mistakes.

Self proclaimed. Eccentric.

Steward who alliterates.

AH C'MON!

If you have lived
A lots of years
And none of them
Are hazy

You're either
A big liar or
Going crazy

If you have never wanted more
than you had
Tried to ignore
That people in your life can
forsake you

Always happy no matter
where life takes you.

Then I'll try not to wake you.

J.S. Christian

Ah C'mon!

MAGNITUDE

magnitude of the impact of complicity on us

80 year old woman had to move to rear of bus

magnitude of the impact of complicity on us

hate crime witnesses don't want to cause a fuss

magnitude of the impact of complicity on us

kids disrespecting elders.
even ok to cuss.

magnitude of the impact of complicity on us

mocking justice with the mindset
"in money we trust"

magnitude of the impact of complicity on us

education dollars so offset no one will dare adjust.

magnitude of the impact of complicity on us

browns missing from the family photo labeled "all of us"

magnitude of the impact of complicity on us

engage alarms then reflex arm because you just don't trust

J.S. Christian

magnitude of the impact of complicity on us

Uniting, Educating, Caring; choosing to discuss

**magnitude of civility when in
God we all trust**

NO FINGERPRINTS

We can't make amends while ignoring
wrongs have been done
or simply choose to forget them

And what is the interest on costs of lives
compounded daily over centuries?

It is a monumental task to piece together
tattered and burned documents
and the promises contained there on.

Do ghosts have rights, fingerprints, or
responsibilities to other ghosts?

J.S. Christian

FAMILY PERFORATION

Try
Hold things
Together.
The left
The right
Or tear right.
Down the

Middle

Only family
Unlike

Family

The only Black.
The only White.
Family perforation

Riddle

J.S. Christian

FISHING TRIP

Stocked lake
Tackle box
Bobber Hooks
Luuuures

Bait
Ties
Cheap beer

Big one!
Suuure...
Catch and Release
Waiting in waders

Ones that got away
Rod
Boat
Reel in
Real fish you caught today.

J.S. Christian

BROWN MASK FAMILY

Brown. Grandma ND, GA, SD
IRR-ish Kreeger CA McPair

Doctor Doctor
Stewart Steward
Officers Duo
MASK Compare

Doctor Doctor
Andersin Andersen
and two brothers
Squared

Dual DNAbled
Hippocratic Oath
Double A Brothers
Bound to Both

Biologically
Historically
Never try deny that we are
Brown Forever Family
Bound Forever, Family
Just ASK

J.S. Christian

PLOTTERS

As you moved closer we thought
you were being friendly
As you moved closer we assumed
that you were kind
Now we can better see
Your steps were only meant to be
used as markers noting
"all of yours is mine"
See exactly where you stand
from where we stood
all of your scales and
measures could
use recalibration.

You were all off.
A misunderstanding
was any cause
for celebration.

J.S. Christian

ARCHIBALD

Everyone seems
Normal within
Their scope of view

Only our outsiders

Find abnormal
What we do

When we scope back
To mirror
All in abutting lens

Then all the little children
See
What crazy really is

NIMBY

You can't see us in the attics
Basements are too dark and dank.
We can't remember how we got here
Though are sure who should be thanked

All the

N.ot-
I.n-
M.y-
B.ack-
Y.arders

J.S. Christian

Wanting us to disappear

We have a right
to have a life and
Live anywhere
but here.

HYPO-

When I stand with my right fist
Held high in the air
While left hand
and fingers
Twirl through my dyed hair.
I cry out "injustice!"
And wide-leg stance stand
Then fob-lock my import and
Sanitize my hands.
After shaking the others' and
Selfie with the crowd
Then post on to Twitter.
These folks are so loud!
I am bailing so hailing a cab
Out of here.
I've done social justice and
Snapped it. Sincere.

J.S. Christian

ALGORITHM CRUSH

It's apparent she has a crush on me

She knows everything I do

She follows me so she can see

just where I am and with who

I wish she would get a life (or a husband or a wife)
So that I could just go on with mine.

I"ve had enough. I will go hit her
"power off!"
Whew! Now I am fine.

DHB

Designated Happy Blacks
Floating big grin smilers
Sometimes unaware
That they are...

The plants of non-supporters
Neither against nor for them
Recruited en route to
somewhere else afar

J.S. Christian

HEIRBORNE

I'm not jumping without a parachute
Or power rockets on my boots
No matter how effing sad I am

Borne. I already aced the test
My beating heart, my breath - SUCCESS!
Even when nobody gives a dayum

Though...

If I forget, can't handle it and
try to quit by winging it
Or make a choice to go out on a limb

Or, out of cash, I dash to splash.
I pray I can remember that
I'm Heir borne.
Thank God I can swim

CONTRACT(UAL)

Take notes to craft a contract with (pathetic) parenthetical voids
Appease to garnish signature. Get funds. Coerce. Destroy
Call meetings then ~~feign fake~~ make emergency on (a parent) time
Then proceed to craft a contract filled with lots a lot of ~~LIES~~ lines
"We will teach your children (not)
enrich their minds
We will be fair (ly) impartial
always nice and kind
(of)
Equal encourage (meant)
will always try to try
Treat all children just the same, ~~except~~ accept disabled".
Why?
Not trusting what was made meant to sound sincere.
"Ignore typos and strikeouts. Just sign here".

FLAVOR

Vanilla with chocolate flavor mixed in
Will never, not ever, vanilla again.
It may not be sweeter it may show no brown
The flavor is inside and always around
Taste may be unnoticed ignored or subdued
Or denied because it is near vanilla hued
Vanilla namesake it if want to pretend
Never not ever vanilla again

144

J.S. Christian

SECRETS

Secrets should be nameless
Since secrets don't exist
Sharing hurts and causes blame
so let's all try resist
If holding is for betterment
then hold, hold on for life
If harming kids, let go of it!
It's Worth the sacrifice.

J.S. Christian

Declarations of Interdependence; Advocate Poetically! square flag is equal4 all sides. 15 stripes, 51-star flag art represents the 15th Amendment Voting Rights. Purple 51st star represents both Purple Hearts and the Washington, D.C. newly **U.nified S.tate of A.merica.**

Advocate Enforcement

WHO HAVE GUNS?

Good guys have guns for bad guys who have guns for good guys who have guns for bad guys who have guns for good guys who have guns for bad guys who have guns for good guys to have guns for bad guys who have guns for good guys guns for bad guys who have guns for good guys who have guns for bad guys Who have guns for good guys to have guns for bad guys who have guns for good guys who have guns for bad guys who have guns for good guys who have guns for bad guys who have guns for good guys who have guns for bad guys who have guns for good guys who have guns for bad guns who have guns for good guys who have guns for bad guys who have guns for good guys who have guns for bad guys who have guns for good

guys who have guns for bad

guys Who have guns for good

guys who have guns for bad guys

who have guns for good guys

who have guns for bad guys

who have guns for good guys

who have guns for bad guys

who have guns for good guys

who have guns for bad guys

who have guns for good guys

who have guns for bad guys

who. .... have guns?

NEIGHBORHOODS

No "White flight" seething quite polite

Vandals destroying all in sight

Blacks in house all day; avoid offend

Goodness is born when thoughts are right

No winners ever in a fight

Just losers of the chance of being friends.

Tiptoeing just makes circles round

Back to the place formerly found

Home where you can raise family with CARE

Imagine if we all could just live there!

JIM, JACK AND STOLI

You, Jim, Jack and Stoli
Should not climb back inside that car
Put the keys down on the bar please
Since you won't get very far
Unless you're willing to
risk killing,
Cars cannot climb up in trees
And little babies strapped in car seats
Can't bear the weight of SUVs.
So you, Jim, Jack and Stoli
Need to vote on what to do
Take the night to sleep it off
Or go hurt a child or two.

J.S. Christian

APPS PD

Appendages aren't perfect
but we definitely
need them
For what it is
in our lives they do.
They are our necessities
light, Order, power, water
which don't work
when cut off
from me and you.

HIGH NOON

I'll bring a rose to your gun fight
So we have to stand at close range
To see Eye 2 Eye
Hoping both can rely
On minds motives and
Moves making change.
Since I'm packing a rose,
please bring water
Since you're packing a gun,
I'll bring pleas
To stand foes-future-friends
Locked and loaded to end
Understanding the
Victor is
PEACE.

J.S. Christian

APB

Put out an
All Points Bulletin
For those suspects who
come packing their ambitions
And full entitlements to

a home, good education, domestic
tranquility,
rights to happiness, due process, life and
liberty,

and any church worship.
With or without steeples.
Put out an ABP for
All Poor Born People.

J.S. Christian

TURN AROUND

When money matters more

Than the people making it.
When animals matter more
than the humans feeding them.
When politics stand taller than TRUTH.
When police have to protect themselves to serve.
**When we say "Shut up!" to justice
and it listens**
Turn Around!

COMPLY

Obey Police:
Don't act combative stupid
Or even think of going up
against the law.
Your friend's car
doesn't drive that fast.

Your cousin's does,
you pay for gas
Then pay with time to say
What you just saw.

J.S. Christian

DROP YOUR WEAPONS

Keep your rounds but drop your weapons.
Keep your fire, pour out the fuel.
Your cannon balls are cute and all
Bandolier look good on you.
Magazines on coffee tables
Make more sense than stuffed in guns.
All can see them there and keep them.

There.
There is...

No damage done.

SAY GRACE

Dear Lord,

Give me grace in the face of fear
So the cops who stop see not race
but hear...
YOUR voice to guide them
YOUR will to give
Merciful kindness
So I can live!

J.S. Christian

Say Grace

OMNIPRESENTLY

When we decide to change how we see
G
O
D
How everything looks will change.

J.S. Christian

JUMPER

Really hate traffic?
Yeah, me too
Even when we cause it
Someone tried to jump off a bridge
So we had to pause it.

NOISES

When you scream I cannot hear you
When you throw I may not catch
The message you're trying to convey
The idea you're trying to hatch
When you stomp,
Reverberations
May crash the bridge
You want to cross.
Your noise may
Get you noticed
But I'm still
boss

J.S. Christian

NATIVE PERSPECTIVE

Fertile, our crops
Evil, your plot.
Your plants grown with our blood irrigation.
Our lives
Your guns
Your germs
You Won.
Our home land became your blood nation.

J.S. Christian

JAKE AND JILL

Jake and Jill went
Up the hill
To fetch some food
And water
Jake fell down
When Jill's dad found
Black Jake out with
his daughter

(AIA) CONUNDRUM

Checks to:

"Ancestral Involuntary Americans"
Shall be drawn from where?

Ghost wages?
Ghost promised land?
Real pain and suffering there?

What about the mules promised?
A mustang car instead?

The classic '62? So, you!

Would you like one in blood red?
Where to deposit reparations
Drawn from ghost accounts?
Would you like the bills distributed
In bones or dirt amounts?

J.S. Christian

ENFORCEMENT GRACE

Dear Lord,
Give me wisdom to serve and protect.
So with every encounter I can project.
YOUR grace patrolling
YOUR mercy maintain.
When force is needed
Restrict or restrain.

DIVINE LIMITATIONS

Sure, there's...
The earth
The moon
The stars
The seas
The trees
And bees
The sun
Oceans and all in between.
Impressive work God's done.
His only limitation seems
He can't leave me alone!

J.S. Christian

ELDERS

We need more old Black men
To teach of cords and chords
Talks with deep wired voices
Sounds with wands and words
Long distance only as far
As uncoiling chords would go
Lessons of strength and knowledge
What the rotary was for.
Professors, Politicians
Who stayed loose,
When things were tight.
Postmen, clergy, papas and
Third job holders by night
We need to have more models
Who're not toddling on the brink
We need more old black men
Before old black men go extinct
History books shouldn't be
The last and only place to see
So we can have old black men,
Can we set young black men free?

172

J.S. Christian

1,2,3 RED LIGHT

Devil Does
Distract
Detract
Divert
Demean
Defeat
Repeat...

ALL HIS

All that I know God taught me
All that I own God bought me
All that I have God gave me
All that I am God made me

J.S. Christian

SINGLE LOADED

Every single day I wake up with the rising sun
Thoughts and prayers are single loaded and do not involve a gun

there's my uniform, my belt, my shoes,
admin blues, my keys

detailed reports stating what is happening on our streets

For all the calls, the codes, the chats, **not a single one will say**

"Take no precautions on the streets; harm innocents today"

THANK YOU

Thank you Lord
For this Day
And every thing
It brings my way
And thank you for
A voice to pray
You'll guide my thoughts
And what I say

J.S. Christian

CHOSEN OUTFITS

The group of us decided before training even began,
That right was right, not Black or White.
Good guys should always win.
Most of us still know the difference.
For all of us, there're judgment calls.
It hurts when bad guys get away

And that the good ones sometimes fall.
We promise. Promise. Promise.
No one signed up to heed a call
other than protect and serve,
protect and serve you
One and all.

CONFESSION

I'm not because I've never been
The guy who keyed your car
The one who flipped you off that time
Outside O'Malley's bar

The guy who poked your tires,
hacked your Calendar. Yawhoo!
Who knew right timing for a vandal.
you'd be gone a day or two

It's just hearsay, never happened
if not seen with your own eyes.
There's not and has never been. A crime.

What cameras?
Oh, crap, you recognize?!

J.S. Christian

Confession

NOT GUILTY

I wasn't even born then
My parents owned no one
I invited most of my classmates
to my parties; out for fun.

I mean, so not everyone could
Come inside my house to play

I could meet them at the local park
And whenever they...

Would invite me over their house
I had something else to do

It was not because of race.
Well, mostly true.

J.S. Christian

PROBABLE CALLS

Dream the day Officer Friendly

is the one who walks a beat

Knows each house, each nosey neighbor.

is the comfort of the street

Little children run out to him

just like an ice cream truck

No one flees or stops having fun.

Even gives a fudge

Ice cream bar to him to share.
He says no thanks.

Stays fit to run.

In case Karen calls and wants him

to come by and scare someone

ENGAGEMENT

"Just try and stop me!"

Oh, I don't have to try
Though I'd much rather you comply.
We both go home to see our wives and kids

"And if I just go?!"

That could actually work.
Less mess, a lot less paperwork
More likely you listened to what was said.

Let's take a breath because we can
Take a moment. Understand.
This exchange has a story that can end.

Something happened, escalated
Did our things, calmly waited
Now praying 🙏 we can just return
To homes as planned.
(man-to-man)

J.S. Christian

JUST LIKE YOU

Groceries
Taxes
Headaches
Heartaches
Backaches
Neighbors
Barking dogs
Kids

Grandkids
Chasing
Hurrying
Worrying
Writing
Daily Logs

DESIGNATED DRIVER

He has so many
Rejections and
Failures
In his life

With college
With career
With finding
A wife

Ending it all
Just seemed
To make
More sense

Though what
Baffled him more
He just couldn't ignore
Was the try-again
Drive was intense

My God, who's
At the wheel
And why do I feel
Accompanied
Just as I'm trying
To quit

J.S. Christian

I can't jump off
To end it
Inspired.
Befriended.
He suddenly
Can just handle it

But why me; the stumbles
Then why not me the jumper
The cliffhanger
Why am I
Even alive?

There were times when
You were designated
To learn
God was designated
To drive

"Yes, cops are just like you"

A REST

We envy them; the seasons
They work 1 quarter of the year
Each one is someone's favorite
Misses them when they aren't here
When they are here few despise them
While out just serving all their best.
We're here all year. We have few fans.
At least they get a rest.

J.S. Christian

BITE YOUR TONGUE

Recall when you
Were very small
A tiny tike
So young

You'd say too much
Incite firm touch
And order
"bite your tongue!"

You're older now
Wiser somehow
Grown discernment
when to stop

Refrain from rage
Never engage
Armed angry
Packing cops

Silence resembles
Solace
Strong ground
Standing ridicule

Have thoughts more
Clear focused then
Drown out angry fools.

Nagging words for
Sayings sake
Sound as
Seething water drops

Beckons wrenches for repairing
send husbands to the roof tops

So sssh...yes, sssh
And listen
For His cue to share your song

Trust you'll have a symphony
And full use of your tongue.

J.S. Christian

STANDING

To pledge allegiance means commitment
standing whatever state you choose.
Take stands on feet or knees,
Wheeled seats
Without influence; win or lose.

Depending on the game,
circumstances or the pain
impact just how pledgers
genuflect
Meditation, silent prayer.
Are also ways to show their
loyalty and the due respect

"The Republic for which it stands"
is those
who heed the call
"Under God
Indivisible
With Liberty
and Justice
for All"

J.S. Christian

NO IDEA

She is here and can hear you
Just no idea what you mean
You are too mean. You are too shiny
Too far away. Not clearly seen.
Come closer, she will zap you
Or slap at you just the same.
Handicapped and harmless. Ask her name.

RIDE ALONG

Officer Mike was on the track team over at Douglass High

He ran pretty fast, finished 4th in his class. A smart super nice guy.

No one was surprised he joined the police force close to his own neighborhood.

Homes, most in shambles, low-incomes; grandmas.
Teens "all up to no good"

Radio: "gang is on the street now not in the local school"
Mike knew importance of education. Importance of following rules

He quickly spots them; just three. He got them.
Staring at Yield and Stop signs.

Something different. Deliberate. Not least bit belligerent.
More awkward than possibly high.

Ready to have to go run after them as police normally did.
But recognized
just looked in the eyes and said
"Hey, what's going on kids ?"

They immediately reached in their pockets and what they pulled out made him laugh

A ruler, protractor, compass for Geometry.
Homeschoolers were out doing Math.

J.S. Christian

ACCESS SUCCESS

One of us in every station
Just lower cabinets; each
Open wider entry doors
Put phones within my reach

Whatever you have to say
Sign or say it to my face

And no matter how tempted you are
Don't take my parking space

DON'T DARE ME

My Dad is a cop.
I'm exempt
from D.A.R.E. class.
If I even
try them
Parents both kick my...

As I was saying, my mother,

J.S. Christian

Cop too
Has promised to kill...

Thoughts of me trying

so I never will
Illegal's illegal.
Why even bother.
Not just because
of my mother and father.

YOU'RE WELCOME

We know if you only knew
what we endure just so you
May have calm and peaceful
sleep at night

There would be a lot less stress.
Civility.
No more protests
and all would certainly act more polite.
We'll do our best
(even thankless)
to promptly answer each and every call.
Rest assured.
You are Welcome one and all.

J.S. Christian

Declarations of Interdependence; Advocate Poetically! square flag is equal4 all sides. The 15 stripes, 51-star flag art represents the 15th Amendment Voting Rights. Purple 51st star represents both Purple Hearts and the Washington, D.C. newly **U.nified S.tate of A.merica.**

Veterans Pray

THANK YOU

Thank you, Lord
for this Day and
Everything
it brings my way
and thank you for a
Voice to 🙏 Pray
You'll guide my thoughts
and what I say

J.S. Christian

LEFT, RIGHT, LEFT

I'm out now which way to turn?

Left

Out instructions on how to earn. Now...

Right

From uniforms to clothes and shoes. Then...

Left

A bunch of memories, cammies and blues. Soo...

Right

After I got out I came to find, I've...

Left

a bunch and best ...me behind.

Right

Now figuring out what's

Left and right to do

When it's not...

Right.What's.**Left**.of.**You**.

J.S. Christian

EXIT STAGE LIFE

The instructions were to be
this way
To eat this way then that
To come this time to
turn back, line up
Never dare get fat

To wear those shoes polish those boots
Still black but make them shine
To march this way and always say that everything is fine

To use our pens
Get issued friends and paper and green socks

You're leaving now so realize the door behind you locks

Keep memories. PTSD. Your children, your ex-wife

No outdoctrination here.
Go. Exit now stage life

HEY OFFICERS

Calling on fellow officers.
Calling on all my men.

(In gender general warrior sense; no intent to offend)

We've a Higher mission calling now. A new non-battle plan.

To use some class, get off our ass and help preserve this land.

I holler from the inside. I don't know the folks out there.

Nor do they apparently.
Imports from everywhere.

Let's wear ball caps to cover; show support of our home teams

(the 40 + amongst us know exactly what I mean)

Not ostracize our allies;.
once cheered with pride

We now sit afar in quarantine instead of alongside

When we regroup, and I know we will, let's all cheer for the same team

Or kiss the things we stood for bye. Pack our things and leave.

J.S. Christian

Me? I'm going nowhere. You should stay your somewhere too.

To lead all by example to get this country through.

I KNOW, not just believe, we can help make things here better

We took an Oath and it's our job to keep the U.S. held together!

BATTLE FATIGUES

The good news is
all are synced
Hard corps ready
in a blink
Battle fatigues
Ready for a fight

But why at home?
We are all one
On the same team
Already done
and too fatigued
to battle now.
No battles now. Gnight.

J.S. Christian

JUST INTRODUCE

Some of us can't walk but still have to get around
others who can't talk are still accountable for sounds
We still need employment empowerment engagement respect
Paid for by funds allotted for same justice all expect
While our moves are different most thoughts and feelings same
Not sure what to say?
Just Introduce
then ask me my name

INTEGRITY

We came from everywhere to here
To support and defend

Our country and all it
stands for.
Make some lifelong friends.

Folks I could trust with my truck, my life security

Due to an oath to be good men of high integrity

J.S. Christian

DEPENDENT

The funeral was very nice
So formal
All were so polite
Lyn wished they could just move
backwards in time

Says their youngest can't remember him
Neither can Lyn mumbling
"Something please take me
back to what was mine"

A soldier, a promise to return.
SGLI was quickly burned and
smoked and sometimes even injected

She coped with dope. Too much wine.
Missing her husband, kids, her mind
Light years from the life she expected.

Before he died, they were on track
Then every single thing went black

She hates the fact they never left Iraq.

J.S. Christian

KNOCK OUT

We've retired.
I know it may sound lame
Let's make some jokes
play memory games

(O-o-o-o-k-a-ay)

Knock-knock

(Who's there?)

"My memory there"

(My memory there Who?)

"So sorry you can't seem recall just who you're talking to."

Knock-knock again
(Who's there)

"There there there there"

(There there there there who?)

"so now looks like your speech's impaired. You also stutter too"

Mind pause then time for
Knock knock 3

(Who's there?)

"Now you've forgotten me?!

Not funny. I don't want to play with you

We were once friends yet in the end you go knock me out too!"

MARCHING ORDERS

Division simply has to die.
We're much stronger when we try
Uniting under one good common cause

It doesn't matter blue or red
or what any shouts or says
Infighting at the very least
should pause

Get the children back in schools
in homes or classrooms
or raise fools

Who think that constant bickering is fine.

The military has it right.
Pick your battles, win the fight.
Know civility is
not a waste of time.

(Trust that God will always lead to do what's right)

OVER THERE

Over there

Over there

We built encampments. We built forts.
Over there
Deflected threats. Cut conflict short
Over there

Over there

Assembled ramps. Assembled towns.
Cleared death camps. Brought evil down.

Over there.

Sharply dressed
Impressed the rest
Showed them all who were the best

Over there.

Now over here...
From over there...

Under duress
Stressed and Depressed

J.S. Christian

Over here...

Fighting Fearing False Arrest

Over here

We love our country.
Love US, Country.

Over here.

ACRONYM SOUP

First DS where we all started from

HOR where we once called home

Zeros in charge who all know.
E's are who really run the show

SOP's giant instruction books
SOB's are ones who always look

follow the book exactly line by line

They get promoted but don't have a real good time

J.S. Christian

THIS ABLED

What we came back with is working just fine
Most of our bodies
All of our minds
Maybe functioning differently.
Altered by time
Impacted by faces and places with mines.

J.S. Christian

GOOD CREDIT

I'm a farm boy from Bismarck
In my town all looked like me

Same people, clothes, hair even noses
As far as eyes
Could see

Marine Corps was very different.

Different as different
could be

It was a big change, at first a tad strange.
Everyone seemed so foreign to me
(so what?!)

Executive Officer, was tough on regimen
He was tall and Black

He taught me always do my best
Hard truths.
Harder facts.

We never got around to race or color. All were green

And rounds are brass won't take a pass if they like how you're seen

Squad leader, Hispanic, was boisterous and strict.

Shared skills how to make it through any conflict

Now out. I'm a successful businessman

Good lessons. Good leaders. Darn good Veterans

J.S. Christian

RECIPROCATE

Do me a favor
Since we served so YOU
Can mock us for simply
choosing to
Defend the country you claim
you love today

Thank a vet, English is still your spoken tongue.
Don't tell any veteran that they do not belong
In your neighborhood
Or on the Gold Star stage

There is no conscript
We chose this path so You
can rest knowing tomorrow too
You can awake and stare freedom in the face.

Reciprocate

In the Civil War
For Civil Rights
During I and II
Full in the fight

J.S. Christian

Korea, and in Vietnam
Then once and
forever
Back at home

Black Lives in Green Matter too

All green when fighting
common foes
Then home *not quite*
as close with bros

Black Lives in Green Matter too

Always for Freedom
Always same cause
Still the same fight
Still the lame laws

Black Lives in Green Matter too

It's not what's in writing
That anyone's fighting

It's hate crimes and so much
condescension that's biting

In housing
in schooling
It's hatred that's fueling
though for you
we'd all risk dying

Black Lives once Green Matter too

J.S. Christian

GOOD GUY

He is not God
so why the
trembling?

He is not God
so why the
fear?

He's just a man
who has no plan

to hurt you.

He's huge,
that's true

Though so
are you

With what it is
you plan to do

To hurt him.

When you call

To cause alarm

See your father

See your son

See our Father and His son

See a man there who has...

No plans to hurt you.

J.S. Christian

DROP YOUR WEAPONS

Keep your rounds but drop your weapons.
Keep your fire, pour out the fuel.
Your cannon balls are cute and all
Bandolier look good on you.
Magazines on coffee tables
Make more sense than stuffed in guns.
All can see them there and keep them.
There.
There is...

No damage done.

NO ONE

I've never known someone of none.
Created from themselves
Conceived from own seed planted, rooted
grown from no one else.
Yet here we are
Adrift
Afar
Aloft
Alone
Astray

No one's some of

Someone's son

Detached then blown away.

J.S. Christian

No One

MUCH RATHER

For the record I'd much rather have
my own house than lay in wait on
a waiting list.
I'd much rather not have to report
To another when I have to take a

Pisses me off when people speak
about but not to me as though I am deaf

I am a person. There is some left.

Don't tease me. Poke at me just ask me my name

Homeless and hopeless look similar aren't same

J.S. Christian

WHENSDAY?

I need to schedule a day for a break down
Next Tuesday at 10 just won't do.
Cause between now and then the subscription* will end.
I don't know if I want to renew
The Monday before is my off day.
Having then would be awkward and bleak.
It would just be absurd
And who's ever heard

Of a breakdown
Beginning the week?
The Sunday before?
Holy heck no!
Guilt alone would just reel me back in.
I'm not baring the cross when
comparing my loss
To life that for me came to an end.
All Saturday I will be solo since the world
takes this day to have fun.
And I'll be here inside
having all day cold cried,
While first responders go bask in warm sun.
Friday 315 is a maybe. Traffic is just starting to slow. Then cause
me all would stop And rush-hour would not.
Rush will be to do, well, we all know.
Thursday 640 could happen.
By then caring friends will all be home.
But, oh wait, no they won't, no they can't, no they don't.

Reality is I have none.
So that just leaves tomorrow and Wednesday The most boring-ist days of them all.
Now have given more thought,
I do know that I ought
go soon humbly and answer this call.
When and if I come back, I'll..

J.S. Christian

HEIRBORNE

I'm not jumping without a parachute
Or power rockets on my boots
No matter how effing sad I am

Borne. I already aced the test
My beating heart, my breath - SUCCESS!
Even when nobody even gives a dayum

Though...

If I forget, can't handle it and
try to quit by winging it
Or make a choice to go out on a limb

Or, out of cash, I dash to splash.
I pray that I remember that,
I'm Heir borne.
Thank God that I can swim

CLUELESS COMPLICIT

I'm pleading not guilty
I committed no crime

The things of your oppression
Happened way before my time

We were forced to look at pictures
of guards enforcing rules.

Now you're
Welcome in all neighborhoods and schools.

Right?

J.S. Christian

API DIVISIONS

We travelled all around the world
Heard foreign languages galore

Learned the proper way to hold chopsticks
in France we learned Amour

Our kids were like celebrities
all Americans the same

Funny pronunciations of
our first and then surnames

Then back home divisions come
with API's and schools

Academic Performance Index

racial sort division tools
The genesis was good we guess.
Monitor our education
now schools use API divides
throughout entire nation

J.S. Christian

PRAYER HELPS

You asked why I Church.
I do it because I can.
It is not the most popular place to go
It's most divine

I go for directions.
It will help to get me home
better than any compass,
map or GPS.

Right now God's
will for me to move
gets me to where others also
Pray and Praise
without judgment.
His will for me to speak
places me in the presence of others
He wills to hear.
Then we switch.
I listen when it's my turn.

We are the two or more
who are
The Church.
So we do.

CHOICES

We choose from our choices
At the altar there was one

The bridesmaids were too giggly
The groomsmen there for fun

My past was far gone history
future present joy
a mystery

And given all choices stated above
I chose the one I love.

J.S. Christian

Choices

PREVENTIVES

Since...

1. Ironically illegal
2. Chance of fail
3. Illogical irrational
4. BFF wails
5. You forfeit rights
6. Kids could see
7. There's tomorrow
8. Your legacy
9. Call incoming from above
10. Your undoing
11. Insult love
12. Insult family
13. Will look odd
14. Deny Heaven
15. Angers God
16. Deny success for foolish fleeing
17. Breathing
18. Seeing
19. Hearing
20. Being
21. Many good things left to do
22. Music
23. Brownies
24. Ice Cream too!
25. Brilliant sunsets
26. Awesome sons

J.S. Christian

27. Walks to take
28. Paths to run
29. Your Country
30. Blessings to count
31. Wealth shared in varied amounts
32. Games to play
33. Games to win
34. Present presents
35. Future friends
36. Doctors
37. Feel. Good.
38. Humor
39. Laughs
40. Clear and str8 and narrow paths
41. Tell-a-vision
42. Selfishness
43. Your Mom
44. Your Dad
45. Erases goodness
46. Reduced to number
47. Go to hell
48. Effing stranger; story tells
49. Whole world sad
50. No way to hide

at least 50 reasons why
NOT to suicide.

think of going long enough,
will get your wish one day.

Not immortal; may be 50 plus away.

FOLD OVER

I try to never confuse
Who I am
With
With
Who I am
They are not the same

J.S. Christian

HMS OUTDOC

He's trying to enter
from rooftops

Simply cannot find
the doors

Stepped out a Higher; Officer.

With no entrance
from bottom floors

Knock Knock

Somebody let me in.

Knock! Knock!

open the door

Let me back in.

Knock! Knock!

Yes, sir

I brought the ships to shore.

J.S. Christian

AESTHETICS

Tourists towns and browns and vets don't mesh. Aesthetics drive away...
Deep pockets who want to come around and, homogeneous, play

This is our home so we belong here. Try to understand.

We shouldn't have to be abroad
to feel American.

HEARTY FARMER

Greg was a hearty farmer with lots of land to care.
Uncomplicated. Unencumbered.
Just wheat and steer out there.
Farm traffic had no stoplights
Tractor drivers never yelled.
He sped 10 miles per hour
rolling
rolling
up hay bales.

To communicate with cattle he didn't have to text
There were never social battles.
He really could care less.
His hearty seeds made feed

J.S. Christian

some vegetables,
for food
and then
He'd grab a hearty handful.
Start the process o'er again.
And again.
And again.

JIM, JACK AND STOLI

You, Jim, Jack and Stoli

Should not
Get back inside that car.

Put the keys down on the bar please
Since you won't get very far

Unless you're willing to risk
Killing
Cars cannot climb up in trees

And little babies strapped in car seats
Can't bear weight of SUVs
So you, Jim, Jack and Stoli
Take a vote
On what to do

Sleep it off and save a life
Or injure
A child or two.

J.S. Christian

TOPS' SECRET

Master Sergeant lead the 'outplacement within 90-day' class

There were nods in agreement
Then the nods of the sleepers

Who just wanted the class to
go fast

At end of the session, the latters, all rested, were pulled to the side by our Top

The talk tone it shifted more intense for the drifters
for what he called
Top's Secret Stop

"You sleep during combat, your soldiers could die!

Rounds make good alarm clocks for men who won't try!

You sleep when you leave here and don't try out there

There's no Tops' Secret stopping to help you prepare.

You get moments not months to transiton; make change.

And much housing and groceries are out of pay range.

These are the hard facts you can not ignore

I gave all of the secrets as you chose to snore

I hope you're well rested from class ample sleep

Go! Take life seriously.
I'll see you next week!"

J.S. Christian

FISHING TRIP

Stocked lake
Tackle box
Bobber Hooks
Luuuures

Bait
Ties
Cheap beer

Big one!
Suuure...
Catch and Release
Waiting in waders

Ones that got away
Rod
Boat
Reel in
Real fish you caught today

J.S. Christian

ENDEARING ENDURANCE

Dear Lord

Know that we are
thankful for
Your Son, the sun,
Faith to endure.
One team of
Difference;
Blessed same
United in your
Holy name
Amen.

J.S. Christian

Declarations of Interdependence; Advocate Poetically! square flag is equal4 all sides.
15 stripes, 51-star flag art represents the 15th Amendment Voting Rights. Purple
51st star represents both Purple Hearts and the Washington, D.C. newly
U.nified S.tate of A.merica.
AMEN

Love

Book VI:
Advocacy for
Love

Declarations of Interdependence; Advocate Poetically! Book VI is Advocacy for LOVE. Love Advocacy acknowledges its varied types and circumstances. Many Americans are engaged in ongoing pursuit of national reconciliation through prayer. Divine love. Can we ever learn to love again?

There are many ways. Traditional Love in a romance "TWINE" and even between Baristas. There is also non-romantic love in a "LOVE 4 COUNTRY CONVENTION" and a song for Red, White, and Blue goldfish.

LIFE IS LIKE

Filled with too much hot air
Bound to float away
Held too tightly

Bound to burst
then nothing left to play
with
Knowing just how little can
control before deploys

Just sit back, go kick back

AND ENJOY!

J.S. Christian

JOY RIDE

i think i'm going to fall

in love

you're giving me a ride...

no I'm not rolling solo.

you are right here

by my side.

since we're riding together,

we have some extra time

to exchange love same,

start changing names

outright out loud outshine

So, yes, no choice

we've bound our voice

No reason and No rhyme.

I may be going to fall in love

with you here by my side

giving me

the company

who also joys

love rides

J.S. Christian

BARISTAS BALL

Kiernan crushed on Keisha.

He just had a thing

for girls with curls
who could make his
warm heart perk and sing.

They were both baristas

at the Coffee Break

Two perfect heart-froth swirlers

Both like lemon cake

Then April, who
Snubbed Frankie,
Crushed on boss
Guy Lee

As did Frankie
who thought himself
More suited for Guy;
Not she.

New girl wrote "yes"
on napkin to Guy
when he sly asked her out

April got mad and
Frankie just laughed
Then dropped his
Tall Chai tea down

J.S. Christian

When Kiernan
found out Kiesha
saw the same
silly thing

He used the story
to get up the courage
to chat, date, then
make her a ring.

TOO OFTEN IN LOVE

Too often in love
We fall.
Hard and fast.
With unyielding hearts
And unhealing bruises
and scars.
Unaware of consequences.
Unbridled and disarmed.
For in this battle
The wounding heartless
Take no prisoners
and tend not to play fair.
Too often in love.

J.S. Christian

INDISCRIMINATE

flames and rounds
are indiscriminate

they take out
what's in their paths

encounters are deadly
imminent
meeting them means
meeting wrath

With heated words
As sharp as swords
Like hatred when
Uncaged

Resulting flames
and rounds are weapons
of the wild rancor
outrage

try love and peace
Discord will cease
and both walk
off the stage

Civility will reign!

LOVE IN MONEY

Let's have U.S.A. civil reunion
In Money, Mississippi

Round up
Multicultural families
Create reparations history

(This is the place we lost Emmett.
Peel off history
still scabby wound)

Time for healing museum for teen boys we (k)need
to come see and reconcile soon

Let's name

"Till Tomorrow"

for Emmett

Since he lost all of his yesterdays

Old men will design it, young men will come build it,

young boys will come help out (and play)

Love brings together.
Time helps heal Forever
Forever and ever
(as it is in Heaven, AMEN)

SOME WHITE MEN

Some White men see
some Black men as
Mysterious
They grow older.
They get bolder and can be
Some White men
who see Black men
as friendly.
Thinking.
We simply view things
so Differently

270

J.S. Christian

SOME BLACK MEN

Some Black men see
some White men as
Complicit.
They grow older.
They get bolder and can be
Some Black men
who see White men
as unburdened.
Thinking.

We view many things
so Differently

LOGIC

It only makes sense
that I love you so much
I've never not.

Freed your heart
Felt your touch
Fed your memories a lot.

It's what we do

Only logical
you love me lots too

TWINE

When you dropped
Down
sprouted roots and
grew on me.
In me
Constant and consistent
over time
Symbiotically changing
Our Hearts'
form and function
receiver to holder
to One of mine

complete and intrusive
permeation growing
Deeper
Tighter
Stronger
Intertwined

Until indistinguishable where
YourYouAndMyMeDivide

I cried.

J.S. Christian

Twine

SKIPPING ROBE

One, two...
Unbuckle our shoes
Three, four
Close the door
Five, six...
Five...six
Five...6
5...
6!
then
Seven, eight
It's getting late
Nine, ten.

        Again.

ODE TO YOU AND POETRY

In this ode to you and poetry
I'm drunk without a drink

Verbose with still an audience
Allowed to overthink

Deep with both deep and shallow
Ends.
Touching without Fingerprints

Though injected and reflected;
Complicated common sense.

Clean immersion in the trenches
High atop with ocean views

And all this just
To get inside of you.

OVERFLOW

Over time
Life brings
more you
and my heart
with you inside it
Beating
Being
Making love
A factory.

I think I'm full to capacity.
and here
you just happen to be
the stimulus for

J.S. Christian

overproduction
and overflow

so you have no...
ok, little,
choice
but to help me in hauling
this surplus of love
I now carry
for you

LOVE COUNTS

Ten years ago we married
Nine years was our fur son
Eight hour days all harried
Seventh year not ton of fun
Six minute miles in marathons enduring time to grieve
Five years of pain and heartache; unable to conceive

Four was the number of times, daily, began to pray
Three in one, Ghost, Father, Son, each and every way

Two years we lie beside and cried. All we could do was done.
One itsy bitsy baby now the three of us are one

J.S. Christian

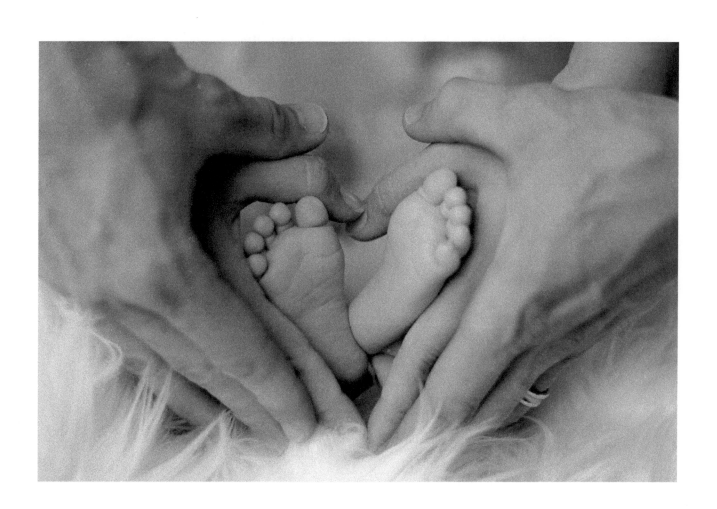

Love Counts

ONE HAND CLAPPING

Bravo for spelling Constitution at just three years old
No limits to what life can reveal as a little life unfolds

Birthday parties: loud annoyances.
Recess: totally unness
Though math and science soothe a soul who math and science best

Periodic table memorized by the age of nine.
A wonderful and wondrous and celebrated mind.

Social studies: felt like waste of time and energy and breath
While thereom proofs wait undefined with little time that's left.

Once it's made official what the youthful genius means
Applauding stops. Invitations drop. Almost immediate. Unseen.

J.S. Christian

One Hand Clapping

FISHY AMERICAN

I am so American
I named my goldfish
Red
White
Blue

My little swimming patriots, so patriotic too
We all know most goldfish don't last for very long
I wax poetic their deaths in fishy patriot burial songs

Red floats hardiness and valor swam from right to left
So strong so brave so upside down so newly now bereft
White purity and innocence; just bobbled well til white
Blue was just and vigilant; he swam from left to right

All come together in the end
fin to fin and glub glub glub
Farewell my brave patriot fish.
you swam so well.
Now Flush!

J.S. Christian

LIKE IS LIKE

Different is easier
Much easier by far

Try saming love
While shaming love

Or faking love
While making love

Only being certain love
Will keep all doors ajar.

Like is Like

SENIORS PROM

Grandma was all gussied up
It had been a while
Since out walking
Friends and family missed her lovely smile
Almost 10 years since grandpa passed seemed like yesterday
til yesterday's
surprise Prom invitation comes Grandma's way
Mike Elder,
a widower himself,
came knocking
(shocking)
and made nosey neighbors peek
seeing these
seniors promenade

together down the street

J.S. Christian

KISSING LESSON

Who in the heck came up with this?
Pressing a face to make a kiss.
The nose knows not what to do
If running somewhere just prior to
The coordination about to begin
How does it start?
When does it end?
Lean in with forehead?
Lead with the chin?

A tilt to side to thwart collide
a nostril and a cheek
Eyes open wide slow pucker glide
to land on lips oblique

J.S. Christian

SOME WHITE GIRLS

Some White girls see some
Black girls as different
They tease them and then both grow up to be
Some White and Black women who should
Befriend
At best and soonest opportunity

TALK PRETTY DO UGLY

Some Natives see all
Non-natives - smooth talkers
They distrust them
and then both
grow old to be
Distant
Disadvantaged
Isolated
Missing alliances and
Growth opportunities

Some Non-natives still see
Natives as mascots
Caricature them
Then say

J.S. Christian

protests seem to be
ungrounded and unfounded
Held resentment
Then plow Native land
from sea to sea.

SOME BLACK GIRLS

Some Black girls see some
White girls as indifferent
They mock them and then
both grow up to be
Some women who should
Befriend. Grow together.
At best and soonest opportunity

J.S. Christian

DOMINIQUE

She seized upon every
opportunity to reveal
the best of herself

by eliminating the worst.
of distractions.
To see certain beauty
There left

Slowly peeling away
The worst features
The worst feeling
The worst fear
The worst name

The peeling away
Then reflection
In turn
Did almost
exactly
The same.

ORIGAMI CLOUDS

I have never seen God's face

I see Him everywhere
Atop Cliffs
pouring water falls
To rivers
In Fresh Air

Shaping clouds
Like origami
Look! There goes a dragon!

J.S. Christian

Right next to a
Bunny pair
Think I hear someone bragging

On everything yet
Still Invisible
Being creating
Love
The author and
The finisher from
Above

STONE COLD

Thank you for sharing all of your warm desires and your dreams
So I can cold more easily align them with my schemes
I always take the time to memorize yours line by line
Have you empty out your quiver then tell you everything is fine
I besmirch your innocence then wink, and smile and blow kisses
slither words over polished teeth forked tongue and slimey hisses
rattler tucked beneath
all muffled Hidden
held silent and tight
then stoned faced

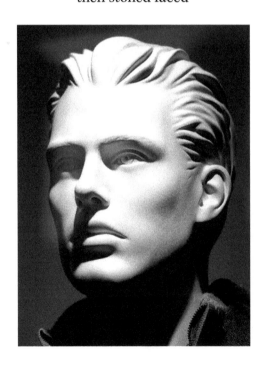

Try to lie with you tonight

J.S. Christian

WE'RE GONNA

If you came
for a fight
We're gonna
Let me show you
my guns

If you came
For a bite
I'm gonna
Get my jacket on

If you came to steal
My heart
Not gonna
It's under lock and key

If you came for love
We're gonna
Have to wait and see

If you're gonna wanna
Fall in love with me

BOOK VII: TRUTH

J.S. Christian

Declarations of Interdependence: Advocate Poetically! 7th book is the artistic iteration of the poetry of real life. Beginning at the "Starting Line" then getting to "Know Santa" along the way.

4 years can seem like 44 marching around in wait
all are related although belated it's never too late
4 this resolution conference for us to finally see the
L.ove
O.rder
R.econciliation (moral)
D.iplomacy

Love of God and self and others
Order and a calm resolve
Reconciliation mindset
Diplomacy: true Moral one

Start at home to show alliance
World reliance happens next
Show our family blood is thicker
Share our **Unity** progress
Unity must be intention if intend walk through the door
Progressed Success past point of venting merely; nothing more
It's time 4 talking
Time 4 listening
Time 4 resolving
Time 4 real care
Weapons held but down.
unloaded.
what happens here is everywhere
and everyone. All men.

What's shot out here hits everywhere.
<u>AMEN</u>

J.S. Christian

STARTING LINE

Since this was his 1st race
in his mind He was 1st place
then he made the mistake
and looked down.

Feet seemed too big.
Confidence quick reneged.
Quicksand seemed
to cover the ground.

Now what should he do?
In a moment or two
the starting gun
would loudly blast.

Think. Think. Think.
Wisen up.
Or fall down in a strut
Rise up always
Fear God; Everlast.

Feet need no directions,
repraise,
introspection
before setting off for a win.

Fixing eyes on the ground
guarantees slowing down.
Wise UP.
Never...
lose your race again.

KNOW SANTA

In his defense
He waited all year
Then waited in

Crazy long lines

No one there dare rush him
He had a long list
And relaying would take
A long time

To see Santa
'Twas Christmas
This is what his gift was
To speak for the deaf
See for blind

He researched all the choices
For ones without voices
For the ones without legs
Who can't climb

Braille books made with mixtures
of smooth and rough textures
With shapes cut to teach
Squares and rounds

And sensory toys
ASD girls and boys

J.S. Christian

Can be easily startled
by sounds

Throw in giant bucket
colorful sidewalk chalk
That's for baby brother
He can't talk or walk

(Kid, others are restless!)
Wish they wouldn't balk!

This isn't for me,
I'll just take world peace
And a little more patience
Behind

Santa said, "I can't bring that.
Kid, you just need Jesus.
He does well with crowds
and long lines"

EVERYTHING

When you try to take
My everything
That matters most to me

I see what of me
Matters
Most to you

These things of your
Obsession
My everythings
Are not possessions

To remove

How can I help you
Help yourself
To move along
Be someone else

Help you seek and
Find
A modicum of
TRUTH

My everything
I willful share
There's room
For all

J.S. Christian

Everywhere!

And for everyone
No need to soul
Remove

No need to sneak
My everything
Is within reach
And hovering

If you want to
take some
Everything
Please do

For Heaven's sake
There's enough
Everything
For you

J.S. Christian

COMPARTMENTALIZED

Love all unconditional
Always face to face

In 4 group compartmentalism
Place

(com-par-wha?!)

1st

For those who know yet love you, Be grateful.

2nd

For unknown admiring strangers, Love them too.

3rd

For former love now grown cold,

try understand something you put them through

4th

For the toughest quadrant, never heed them.

Never provoke. They dip. You stay above.

They're trite. Don't trust.
This group we must...

Love.
Yes.
Love.
Yes.
Love.
Yes.
Love.
Yes.
Love.

These malcontents are
currently our neighbors,
our pretend friends, our outcast; misinformed

They've jealous hearts and fear of making missteps
Be sure to always face
with open arms

J.S. Christian

LULLA-BYE

We are all so different
How can we pull it off
Pulling everyone together
Ending strife

Find the lyrics
That will go
To the tune of songs
We know

To sing
Of joy
To sing
Of Him
To sing
Of Life

Let's la la la our
Way to it
We have no choice
But bound through it

Or sing the goodnight
Country la la bye

TONI

Toni is the
epitome of regal

Cool calm collected
Keeps wits about her
Through the storm

She knows
No matter where
No matter when
No matter what
Or how

She can always
Reach and grab
Her Father's arm

Toni

REAL

I don't slip into this skin by day
Take it off at night
Pretend to be your friend;
And grin
To help you seem polite

I'm not wearing latest bodysuit
Yes, color is in style
Dermatologically
It's me!

And I refuse to smile

At night so you can
See me -ha!
Joke got old when
It was new

Won't sing or dance
Partake parlance
Though I will
pray with you

And I will pray for you!

J.S. Christian

BITE YOUR TONGUE

Recall when you
Were very small
A tiny tike
So young

You'd say too much
Incite firm touch
And order
"bite your tongue!"

You're older now
Wiser somehow
Grown discernment
when to stop

Refrain from rage
Never engage
Armed angry
Packing cops

Silence resembles
Solace
Strong ground
Standing ridicule

Have thoughts more
Clear focused then
Drown out angry fools.

Nagging words for
Sayings sake
Sound as
Seething water drops

Beckons wrenches for repairing
send husbands to the roof tops

So sssh...yes, sssh
And listen
For His cue to share your song
Trust you'll have a symphony
And full use of your tongue.

J.S. Christian

ADULT TREE

Cherry trees have cherries
Peach trees bear their name

Apple trees content vary
Fig trees mostly look the same

They all begin as saplings
Grow into something sweet

All good with temping goodness
All except the Adult Tree.

It is pretty. It grows poisonous.
It has Branches. It grows vines.

Adult Tree first bites seem delicious
Whither insides over time

So have a peach, cherry or apple
Folded warm inside a pie

A much sweeter post repentance
You can't deny

BAD GUY

For the record, we are created
then make choices as we grow

Some of them are good ones
the rest are, well, you know.

The good ones are applauded
Will be lauded. Smiley shared

The others sit in darkness

Lanquished
Guilty
Frowning
Scared

J.S. Christian

Your thoughts they're known
Your heart it's shown
Your ways revealed. Defiled.

Light shines clear through
the real you
In a matter of time.

The good news is it can end well, to some it may seem odd

You can rely bad ways can die.
Repentance lives.
Ask God.

MATHEMATIC SOLUTION

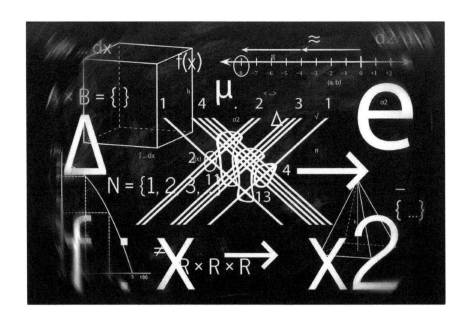

Hate times hate
Is hate squared
Times one more hate
It's cubed

Multiplied
It replicates
Regurgitates
Renewed

J.S. Christian

Hate added
Just reflects itself
Division
Does the same

Subtracting
Is the only way
That hate
Can be contained.

KIN FOLK

He didn't ask
To come here
She didn't make
Herself born

Different Mothers and
the same Dad
Different fathers and
same Mom

Acknowledged or not
as same family
DNAbled.
No Judgment.
No end.

No life is created
in error
Not
Coincidentally
Chosen
As Kin.

J.S. Christian

WATERWAYS

When I drink the water
I don't analyze the elements
I'm dry and water's wet
To quench my thirst

Can't taste 2
hydrogen
Hydrations

One oxygen
Oxygenated

Only recalling that the parching
was there first

Likewise a spirit
Can get dried out
Fears and tears all
Can get cried out

Earthly elements can offer
Only grief

So choose to take it
Higher
Drink the word to
douse the fire

Cool the flames with
Holy Waters of belief.

324

J.S. Christian

PET PEEVES

Proudly looking

over the mess

he planned and

ran to evil do

styrofoam blood

from teddy bear

Wicked agenda

For those shoes

Denied (yea Lied) he knew of it
Then hung his head in shame

Claimed the cat and gerbil did it
Causing discord with the blame

Seven!
Committed all
Of them
Promise
Never do again!

Thank God
Pets aren't
accountable
(Like us humans)
when they sin.

J.S. Christian

ALLEGED IMPOSTER

You've earned every
Right to sit there

You've done far more
than them to get here

from your home.

yet you sit amongst
the crowd

very much alone

The peacocks
Display their plumage
The legacies
All lineage up

The Entitled
Around whom
The Universe was
Formed

(Also have
Imposter Syndrome.
It is the norm.)

You've earned every
Right to sit there

You've done far more
Than them to get there

On your own; alone.

(you're not alone)

J.S. Christian

WHYT

I'm White

I am not the boogie man

I don't feel privileged

Understand

My understanding's

From my point of view

It's tough to feel

When never touched

I'll try to do this better

MUCH

I may need Empathy

From You

And you

You too.

J.S. Christian

RECEIPTS

The White House

Your peanut butter
jelly sandwich

The separation of a set
of Siamese twins

Lights. The incandescent
And ones for traffic.

Smooth real McCoy inside
Of train engines

Your freedom."Georgias",
Super soaker Waterguns.

Entertainment and the
Talent sources from

Electrical resistor
Laser cataracts removal

Receipts for what some
Brown people have done

USS ALLYSHIPS

Allyships can help us
Sail across the waters

Invite inside to
See how vessels
Work and run

Over the waters
Through the rough
seas far too choppy
Life can be sloppy
Once the living has begun

Mentors map the
Path and sing
Song same semantics
Model, motivate to join
Out on the floor

Allies share the keys
Unlock right doors;
swing
Open

Opportunity awaiting
on the shore

J.S. Christian

HIGH TAXES

In California you
Pay more to see
The ocean

In Colorado you
Pay more to
Ski the slopes

In New York
Land near Central
Park is premier

In Texas they
Pay taxes
Just to boast

In the U.S.
Take a wild guess
Just who is
Taxed the most

The disabled
Just for being
Coast to coast.

J.S. Christian

WHAT'S THE WORD

It's laughable how easily our memory declines

Forgetting proper words for things happens all the time

What's that stuff around the tree

That's brown and textured. So pretty?

And keeps them covered in daylight

As well as in the dark of night?

it's bark!

What's the word, it rhymes with Jim

That holds up flowers ?

It's a stem!

Yeah, kinda close. I need a hint.

Is it the integument?

Or integumentary?

It surrounds, supports,

US - varied?

Community!

Super close, can clearly see

You are thinking...

Family!

Eureka!

Maybe just 1/2 guessed

God and Families

gets the YES

D. J.

Jay saw the flyers

Needed some music

As no party is complete

Without music everybody

will just sit bored

In their seats

Jay asked Him, can you D.J. my party?

I like your music. Your groove

Can you help me out
Then get them up
Help my whole party move?

D. J. then considered the offer

Drafted clear concise contract

"I'll take this gig if you agree

To give me all my due respect

And tell your friends,
they condescend and
I will quickly pack

No racist jokes
From any folks
No matter White or Black

Let's together make a praylist
Some of yours. All is mine.

Creating new is good for you
Let's go have a real
Good time!

Don't Judge me.
And you can see
This party's up and
off the wall

Working TOGETHER
Good times
Can be had by ALL!

J.S. Christian

SNACKS

In November the season
Of snacking begins

Leftover candy, food frenzy
No end

The parent tradition
Hide sugary snacks

The kid premonition
Try get around that

Box stacked 4-2-1
in a pyramid

Just strong enough to hold
snack sneaking kid

Not wise enough to know
Fathers keep eyes

Out for snack sneaking
And box stacking tries

Aware of all efforts
So funny so far

(Replace sweets;
Flax granola bars)

J.S. Christian

TRUTH IN LIFE

BEAUTIFUL IN LIGHT

SAVE SUPER WOMAN

Kay knows she has to save
the world.
She also has to eat.

This means she has to
skip a meal or two

And skip
Her sleep
And skip
Heart beats

Since she skipped time to
Stay Healthy;

Imbue

The cape needed washing
Prosecutors case squashing
Taxes would not file themself.

Cause call never questioned
Nor the fact she was best at
Though the worst at
How and when to shelf

Wondrous humble mighty fortress
find time and place to put aside

The armor breastplate
mask sword and cape
relax and imbibe

Super woman
Super take care
Of yourself!

U.

S.

A.

UNIFIED

State of America

What does the flag cover art symbolize?
Middle school art project winner. Declarations of Interdependence; Advocate Poetically! The equal
4all sides square flag equals 15 stripes to represent Voting Rights 15th Amendment. There are
51 stars. The 51st purple star represents Purple Hearts, (bipartisan Washington, DC) and the
U. nified S.tate of A.merica

CPSIA information can be obtained
at www.ICGtesting.com
Printed in the USA
BVHW021938291220
596561BV00018B/1818